WEDDING SONGS
of Love and Friendship

M000107812

CONTENTS

Photo credit: Fred Sieb Photography

HAL•LEONARD™
CORPORATION

7777 W. BLUEMOUND RD. P.O. BOX 13819 MILWAUKEE, WI 53213

BECAUSE

Words by EDWARD TESCHEMACHER
Music by GUY D' HARDELOT

ALWAYS

Words and Music by MICHAEL W. SMITH
and GARY CHAPMAN

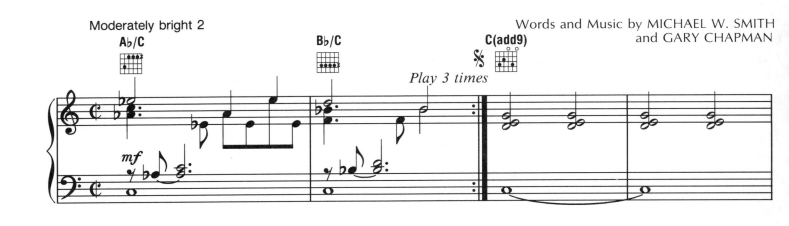

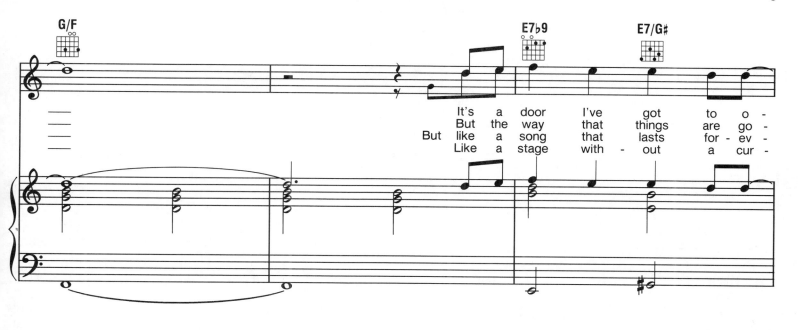

It's a door I've got to o -
But the way that things are go -
But like a song that lasts for - ev -
Like a stage with - out a cur -

- pen, a ship that's got to sail
- er, with a cho - rus from now on, to the
you have

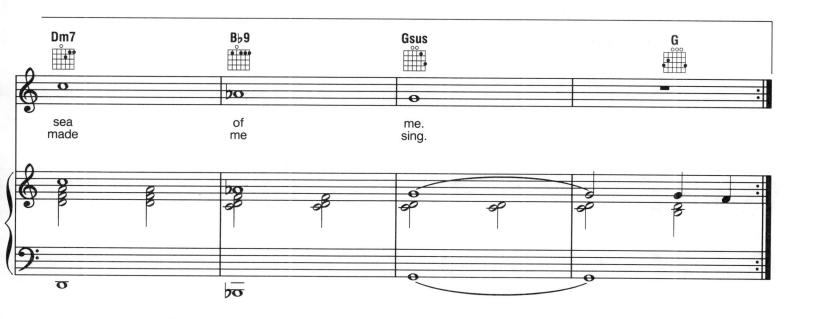

sea
made
of
me
me.
sing.

ARMS OF LOVE

Words and Music by GARY CHAPMAN,
MICHAEL W. SMITH and AMY GRANT

BRIDAL CHORUS
(From "Lohengrin")

RICHARD WAGNER

DOUBLY GOOD TO YOU

Words and Music by
RICHARD MULLINS

Moderately

15

FRIENDS

Words and Music by MICHAEL W. SMITH
and DEBORAH D. SMITH

Pack - ing up___ the dreams___ God plant - ed
With the faith___ and love___ God's giv - en

In the fer - tile soil___ of you;___
Spring - ing from___ the hope___ we know;___

HE HAD IT PLANNED LONG AGO

Words and Music by
ANDREW CULVERWELL

27

HERE WE ARE

Words and Music by
DALLAS HOLM

29

HOUSEHOLD OF FAITH

Words by BRENT LAMB
Music by JOHN ROSASCO

Here we are___ at the start,___ com-mit-ting to___ each oth-er___ by His Word and from our hearts,

Now to be___ a fam-i-ly___ we've got to love___ each oth-er at an-y cost un-self-ish-ly;

IN THIS VERY ROOM

Words and Music by
RON and CAROL HARRIS

I AM LOVED

Words by WILLIAM J. and GLORIA GAITHER
Music by WILLIAM J. GAITHER

With conviction (not too fast)

1,2. I am loved, I am
3. loved, you are

loved, I can risk lov-ing you For the
loved, You can risk lov-ing too, For the

One_____ who know me best loves me most.
One_____ who knows you best loves you most.

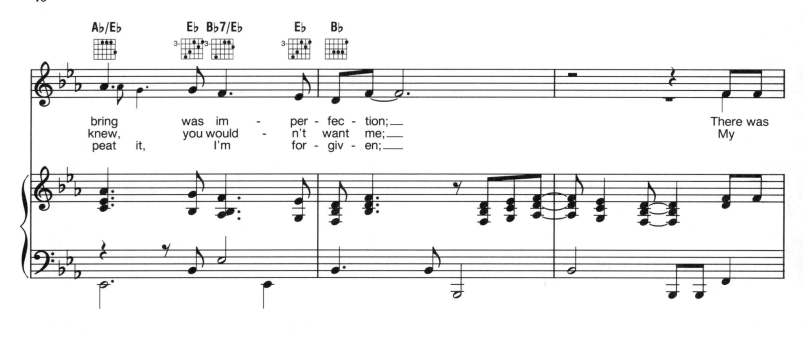

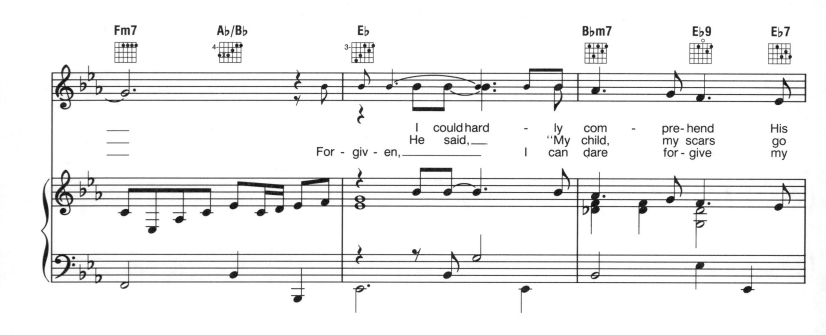

I COULD NEVER PROMISE YOU

Moderately

Words and Music by
DON FRANCISCO

I could nev-er pro-mise you ___ on
(Verse 2: See additional lyrics)

just my strength a - lone. ___

That all my life I'd

care for you ___

and love you as my

Verse 2

But the love inside my heart today
  is more than mine alone;
It never changes, never fails,
  and it never seeks its own.
And by the God who gives it
  and who lives in me and you,
I know the words I speak today
  are words I'm going to do.

LET'S KEEP GROWING

Words and Music by
ROBERT CULL

LET US CLIMB THE HILL TOGETHER

Words and Music by
PAUL CLARK

THE LORD'S PRAYER

By ALBERT HAY MALOTTE

LONGER

Words and Music by
DAN FOGELBERG

64

65

MORE
(Theme From MONDO CANE)

English Words by NORMAN NEWELL
Music by RIZ ORTOLANI and NINO OLIVIERO

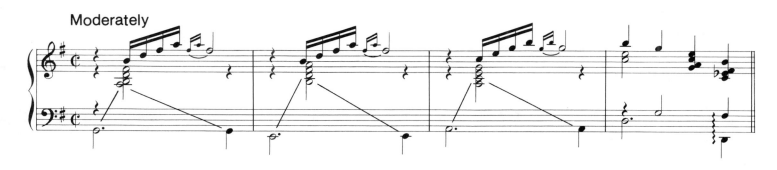

More than the great-est love the world has known;

This is the love I'll give to you a - lone.

ME AND MY HOUSE

Words and Music by
TIM SHEPPARD

SUNRISE, SUNSET
(From the Musical "FIDDLER ON THE ROOF")

Words by SHELDON HARNICK
Music by JERRY BOCK

Moderately Slow Waltz Tempo
(soulful and wistful)

PORTRAIT OF LOVE

Words and Music by KENNY WOOD
and BILLY CROCKETT

TILL THE END OF TIME
(Based On Chopin's Polonaise)

Words and Music by BUDDY KAYE
and TED MOSSMAN

Slowly, with expression

Till The End Of Time,_____ Long as stars are in the blue_____

_____ Long as there's a spring, a bird to sing I'll go on lov - ing

TOGETHER

Words and Music by
LYNNE BROWER

88

TRUE LOVE

Moderately Slow

Words and Music by
COLE PORTER

WEDDING MARCH

FELIX MENDELSSOHN

Majestically

WE HAVE THIS MOMENT, TODAY

Words by GLORIA GAITHER
Music by WILLIAM J. GAITHER

hand   as   we   run   through the sweet   fra -   grant mea - dows,   Mak - ing
My   lit - tle   son   run - ning there   by_____   the hill - side   may
near   while they're here,   And   don't   wait   for   to - mor - row,   to

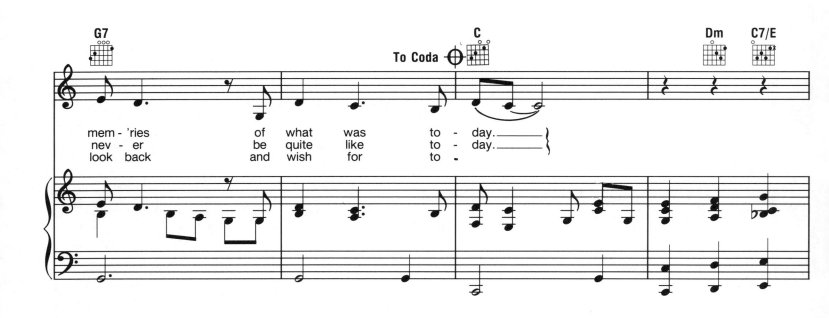

mem - 'ries   of what was   to - day.____
nev - er   be quite like   to - day.____
look back   and wish for   to -

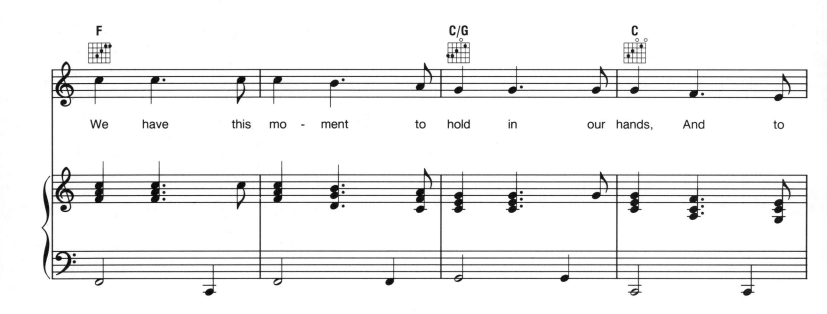

We have   this mo - ment to hold in our hands, And   to

G7 C G7 C7
touch as it slips through our fin - gers like sand;
F C/G C
Yes - ter - day's gone, And to - mor - row may nev - er come, But
G7 C 1 G7 2 G7
D.S. al Coda
we have this mo - ment to - day. Tin - y Ten - der
CODA C A♭7 D♭ D♭maj7
day. 4. Take the blue of the sky and the

WEDDING PROCESSIONAL
(From "The Sound Of Music")

Words by OSCAR HAMMERSTEIN II
Music by RICHARD RODGERS

Majestically

For the entrance of the Bride

WHAT A DIFFERENCE YOU'VE MADE IN MY LIFE

Words and Music by ARCHIE JORDAN

WEDDING PRAYER

Words and Music by
FERN G. DUNLAP

112